Naima Mora Model Behavior

Copyright © by Naima Mora.
All rights reserved. Published in the United States. No part of this book may be used or reproduced in any manner whatsoever without express written permission except in the case of breif quotations embedded in articles or reviews. For information address official Naima Mora website www.naimamoraonline.com

SECOND PRINT EDITION PUBLISHED 2013

Library of Congress Cataloging-in-Publication Data
Mora, Naima
Naima Mora Model Behavior.
2nd print edition ed.p.cm
ISBN 978-1493755288
1. SELF-HELP/Motivational & Inspirational. 2. SELF-HELP/Personal Growth/Success. 3. HEALTHY & FITNESS/ Healthy Living. 4. BODY, MIND & SPIRIT/ Inspiration & Personal Growth.

NAIMA
MODEL BEHAVIOR
A LITERARY EXPERIENCE BY NAIMA MORA

FOR ALL THOSE WHO HAVE SUPPORTED ME.
FOR MAHALIA, MY SISTER MY JEWEL ...
AND FOR SOFIA, NOAH, NIYA AND AZA
WITH LOVE,
NAIMA

NAIMA
MODEL BEHAVIOR
A LITERARY EXPERIENCE BY NAIMA MORA

EDITED BY
KATHRYN MATTINGLY

COVER PHOTOGRAPHY BY
NIA MORA-MOYNIHAN

GRAPHIC DESIGN BY
NIA MORA-MOYNIHAN
&
NAIMA MORA

PHOTOGRAPHY THROUGHOUT
SEE CREDITS

Forward

I have had the fortune to know some pretty incredible women. These women are my peers, friends, and sisters. They are some of the most beautiful and talented women I have ever had the honor to meet and have be apart of my life. They are all talented, creative, beautiful, kind, honest and nuturing friends. I realized not too long ago that these young women have helped and suported me throughout my darkest hours, inspiring me to have courage and continue persevering towards accomplishing my dreams. I have felt an insurmontable amount of appreciation and gratitude for each of them. It is because of them I have decided to write this book.

I wanted to write something both encouraging and inspiring for young people. Something simplistic and beautiful to remind them that success and confidence lies within the simple idea that you really can achieve your dreams - with hard work and belief in your own limitless potential and individual beauty.

When I started modeling, I had just won America's Next Top Model and was struggling with my own sense of beauty and confidence. I had experienced the ups and downs of the fashion industry and years later am now able to recognize the postive and negative effects it had on my life.

Modeling can be a very glamorous job, it can also be very dark and lonely. I wanted not to perpetuate the negative connotations associated with modeling (a lot of which I had expereinced first hand), but offer young people the perspective that they too can lead a glamorous life. I wanted to write about this perspective based on my positive experiences as a model and the amazing lessons I have brought with me along the way. Reality Television has become a Pop fad in our culture, allowing many people to become famous overnight. A person's self worth is often determined by whether or not they are famous via television or have otherwise become a viral sensation. I want to offer something real behind my experience in reality TV, as in how to be true to one's self once the lights are off and the cameras are no longer rolling. I really want young people to believe in themeselves and their own idividual beauty. I want them to find glamour in it.

Finally, in writing this book, I hope to encourage the creativity, compassion, love and humanity we all have innately within our lives- by expressing my own.

table of contents

CHAPTER ONE
A PIECE OF MY HEART   PAGE 1

CHAPTER TWO
BECOMING BEAUTIFUL;
RELATIONSHIPS   PAGE 13

CHAPTER THREE
EXPLORING YOUR SOUL   PAGE 31

CHAOTER FOUR
MODEL DIET   PAGE 55

CHAPTER FIVE
RULES TO LIVE BY   PAGE 83

CHAPTER SIX
PICTUE PERFECT   PAGE 97

CHAPTER SEVEN
FOR YOU   PAGE 127

CREDITS   PAGE 135

chapter one
a piece of my heart

the salt of tears

I stood there naked. Removing the blindfold by slowly and painfully opening my heavy eyelids, I stared at my bare reflection. Stoically, almost in a trance, I dissected every piece of me.

My feet on the cool floor, hands to my side, swaying to a motionless wind, I was preparing to receive the rain of sharp bullets pouring in from the firing squad of my own critical gaze. With slow, short, shallow breaths, I was preparing to take inventory of every flawed part of me, which happened to be all of me. I loathed what I saw and what I felt. The sharp edge of my glare had begun to cut me open, examine and probe at my viscera.

I could feel it all slipping away. Painfully it was running through my fingers. It was falling through my grasp - life, love, sanity. Like sand, my hold on reality was spilling away one grain at a time. I had done this ceremony of self-sacrificing thousands of times, but it was only at this moment I realized how often. Could I have really disliked me so much? Was this what rock bottom felt like? This wasn't supposed to be happening to me. Everyone told me how I had everything and was so strong. What happened? How did I get here?

The air was hot and motionless, but my skin prickled and chilled my flesh. I was spun up into memories of things that had happened to me - of my parents divorce, of my first of anxiety attack at eleven, of friends lost too early, of growing up poor, of seeing what poverty does to people, of not feeling good enough or worthy enough to accomplish my dreams, of racism and sexism, of bad relationships, of all my relationships (love or friendships) failed due to abuse, of sacrificing integrity for something called beauty, of moving to New York

AT EIGHTEEN, OF FIGHTING WITH MY PARENTS, OF BEING KICKED OUT AND RUNNING AWAY, OF FEELING LOST AND UNCERTAIN, OF HIDING BEHIND DEBAUCHERY OR SELF-MEDICATION THROUGH SOMETHING CALLED FUN, OF SELF-ABUSE, OF SMILING WHEN I'M HURTING, OF PRETENDING TO BE HAPPY WHEN I'M NOT.

WHAT WAS LEFT BUT BURNING TEARS? THERE WAS NOTHING ELSE I COULD DO AT THAT MOMENT BUT CRY. MY FRAGILITY HAD FINALLY CAUGHT UP TO ME. I'D SPENT YEARS BEING THIS ROCK OF A HUMAN BEING, STRONG AND DETERMINED AND NOW I FELT LIKE I HAD BEGAN TO CRACK FROM THE BRUTALITY OF LIFE BEATING UP ON MY FREE SPIRIT.

ALONE, I STOOD RIPPING MYSELF TO PIECES BECAUSE THAT WAS THE ONLY WAY I KNEW HOW TO REACT. I WAS BEING HARD ON MYSELF, BECAUSE WHAT THAT USUALLY MEANT, WAS THAT I WAS MY TOUGHEST CRITIC, AND THAT I WAS SUPPOSED TO GROW FROM SUCH HARSH CRITICISM. BUT THIS WAS FAR FROM CONSTRUCTIVE, IT WAS QUITE THE CONTRARY, IT WAS DESTRUCTIVE.

"yesterday makes me who I am,

Where had I forgotten how to nurture myself? Where had I forgotten how to cradle the love in my heart and to nourish my dreams? Where had I forgotten that yesterday makes me who I am, but does not define who I can become?

What was left now but my tears? I could taste their salt in my mouth, parching my throat. There was nothing else I could do at that moment but wipe my eyes, and inhale and exhale. Rub away the tears I had never allowed myself to cry. Alone, I stood there and realized that I was the only person standing in my way of love and success. I realized that I, and I alone, have all the power and control to change my fate. For the first time in a long time I made the decision to like me for all that I was, and it was really hard. But I could nurture my feelings and cradle the love in my heart. I could get out of the way of myself and allow me the chance to follow my dreams.

but does not define who I can become"

life is a gift

I truly believe in the potential of human beings. I believe with all my heart that people are capable of amazing feats. In my life I have seen countless examples of this in the lives of people. Think about all your heroes and heroines, people you look up to and truly admire. Look at all that they have accomplished. What separates them from you is nothing except their successes, which you are fully capable of accomplishing with a lot of hard work and belief in yourself.

I grew up in Detroit. My family wasn't well off financially. Since the fall of the automobile industry in the 1960's Detroit has had some of the highest statistics in the United States for murder and other violent crimes, as well as illiteracy rates. As children, my sisters and I were witnesses to a large amount of violence. It was a rough city to grow up in. I had to look beyond my circumstances and up to my heroes for inspiration. With my free spirit, I really didn't have a choice but to adopt one very important idea, "If they could do it, I can do it!"

However so, it's hard to entertain the thought of becoming successful at what you really love doing once the notion of **RESPONSIBILITY** settles in. Most people believe that they have to follow the progressive guidelines for a normal life: childhood, high school, college, job, marriage, children. Nowhere in those guidelines is there room for entertaining what it is they really want to do and, sad to say, most people forget what it was they wanted altogether! Or more sadly, they're never given the opportunity to find out.

Every man and woman has the potential to create something magnificent. Life is a gift for discovering what manifestation our talents can leave behind whether physical, mental, or emotional. I want to share my personal journey towards this realization. By empathizing with my story, perhaps I can help each of you to find your true potential for love and for pursuing your own dreams in life.

chapter two
becoming beautiful; relationships

Every facet of my career be it dancing, modeling, or singing, has had a high focus on image, esthetics and beauty. 'Beauty' is a tricky word and sometimes a very confusing idea. The popular idea of 'Beauty' in the impressionistic minds of developing youth can often lead to negative body image and a very self-critical internal struggle. I have learned throughout my career that with the help of artists and highly trained professionals, I, a regular girl from Detroit, Michigan, can be turned into an Amazonian bombshell — something iconic in the present popular idea of 'Beauty.'

On a day-to-day basis, I prefer being in jeans and t-shirts with no make up on at all. After the transformation of a photo shoot however, I become a completely different person. In short, the idea of 'Beauty' in pop culture has become an illusion that artists within the industry have the power and ability to manipulate. 'Beauty' is really an elusive concept, changing and transforming through the various interpretations of artists, media and pop culture. Most people are unable to separate their own understanding and definition of what is 'Beauty' from how the media, pop culture and various artists define it.

When I Grow Up I Want To Be.... Beautiful?

I knew that I always wanted to be a performer! If you think back to your happiest memories as a child, it can give you a hint as to what you truly love and what you are meant to do in life. My happiest memories are of my family, being athletic, and being a performer... a **STAR**! At age ten I would spray paint old vinyl records that belonged to my mother and make special labels on them that read 'This Gold Record Is Hereby Presented to Naima The Great.' I would then present the awards to myself, frame and hang them on my bedroom wall. I was only ten years old and already winning gold records!

When I got really serious about making a career choice in the performing arts at sixteen, I didn't realize I would need to fit into someone else's idea of 'Beauty' in order to be successful. I didn't realize then that I was already beautiful, just the way I was. Thereafter, I started believing that I was never truly beautiful because I wasn't born in the image of someone else's definition of 'Beauty.' I didn't naturally have long flowing hair. Mine is fuzzy and has a tendency towards becoming an unruly Afro. I wasn't a size two when I wanted to become a ballet dancer and a model. I was a size nine. I didn't look typically 'beautiful.' I had exotic features.

With that misdirected understanding of 'Beauty' and with the turns of life such as my parent's divorce, numerous relationships gone bad, and the regret of reckless things I'd done that I am not too proud of, I came to the conclusion that I was unbeautiful and undeserving of love. That I was not even deserving of my own love. I continued to be reckless, living life wildly to escape the inner disdain I had for myself. I had little regard for anyone or anything but was consumed by this void called lovelessness.

After living with this inner turmoil for years, I seemed to have ruined every relationship I had encountered. I was on bad standing with everyone, including myself.

But there is only so much of this self-loathing that the human heart can take. We need to love, we need to be loved, and the really fascinating part of the whole thing is that we are always loved by God, the Universe, a Higher Power or whatever you choose to call it. I may have forgotten this, but my heart did not. If I was truly going to begin filling my life with purpose again, I had to begin by rebuilding the relationships I had broken. Rebuilding a good relationship with me was the first thing I had to conquer. I never gave up on my dreams, but for a while there, I may have given up on myself. Now had come the time to fix that. And trust me, with a lot of hard work and belief everyone can fix this.

Me, Myself...
and EVERYONE ELSE!

I LEARNED TO TAKE A STEP BACK, ASSESS WHAT IS REALLY GOING ON IN MY LIFE AND BECOME TRULY HONEST WITH HOW I FEEL ABOUT IT. WITH HONESTY COMES RESPONSIBILITY. I'VE LEARNED TO ACCEPT MYSELF AGAIN AND TO BECOME PATIENT WITH WHO I AM AS A PERSON AND WITH THOSE THINGS IN THE PAST THAT HAVE SHAPED ME. I HAVE HAD TO TAKE RESPONSIBILITY FOR MY ACTIONS, ESPECIALLY THE ONES I'M NOT PROUD OF. ONCE I BELIEVED THAT I COULD CHANGE HOW I FELT ABOUT MYSELF I REALIZED THAT CHANGING MY ATTITUDE WAS THE FIRST STEP.

I HAD TO BECOME POSITIVE ABOUT MYSELF, MY LIFE, AND EVERYTHING IN IT. I HAD TO BECOME A LITTLE MORE EASY-GOING. I WAS SO USED TO HARBORING NEGATIVE SENTIMENTS, HOLDING GRUDGES, AND HOLDING ONTO PAINFUL MEMORIES OF THE PAST, THAT BEING POSITIVE WAS VERY DIFFICULT AT FIRST. BUT AS JANICE DICKINSON ONCE TOLD ME, "FAKE IT TIL YOU MAKE IT!" SMILE EVEN WHEN YOU DON'T FEEL LIKE IT AND OVER TIME IT WILL BECOME GENUINE. I LEARNED TO FIND BEAUTY IN THE SIMPLE THINGS AND I MADE A CONSCIOUS DECISION TO NEVER FEEL SORRY FOR MYSELF OR GIVE IN TO FEELINGS OF SADNESS.

I love being a social person and for a long time, being social and 'out on the scene' meant losing touch with my inner feelings. With my newfound honesty however, I realized that being a social butterfly is not always the best thing for me. Sometimes, maybe what's best for me is staying in and relaxing at home and being creative, or going to a movie, or reading a book. Maybe it's visiting with one close friend, rather than five hundred close friends. I had to be honest with myself about what would truly make me happy at the moment rather than allowing myself to fall into old behavior patterns that had led to my unhappiness.

Taking a short hiatus from my large social network and focusing on myself allowed me the time to reflect upon other relationships in my life- my family, friends, and 'friends.'

First of all, I began to understand that I have always had my family, who would be there for me through anything. Then I had my friends. I mean real friends that have loved me for me throughout all my phases of life. Friends I could call to bail me out, and

CONTRARIWISE. THESE WERE THE PEOPLE THAT I COULD NOT IMAGINE LIVING WITHOUT. AND LAST OF ALL, I HAD MY OTHER 'FRIENDS.' PEOPLE WHO WERE COOL TO HANG OUT AND PARTY WITH, AND WHO WERE REALLY FUN, BUT WHO, AT THE DROP OF A DIME, WOULD ALSO LEAVE ME DESERTED IN THE MIDDLE OF hell without a drink of water. After characterizing the people I had in my life, I had to determine how I was going to salvage the relationships that mattered most to me. I also had to determine how was I supposed to get over the anger I felt for 'friends' I had allowed to abuse me.

I came to this conclusion: All people go through the same emotions and learn the same things at different points and in different ways throughout their lives. We are pretty much all the same, and after I began seeing people in this light, I understood how to respect them as equals and how not to judge them or myself. I learned to accept people for who they are, not who I wanted them to be. A lot of times we are expecting prince-charming to prance into our lives, whisk us away and live happily ever after in some far off land of make-believe. This idea even extends to our family and friends. We expect people to be perfect. But people have flaws and that makes us all different and individually beautiful. No one is ever going to live up to the standards you may hold for them and when we drop these standards we allow our friends and our family to love us the best way THEY know how.

With this idea in mind you have control over your relationships. When someone shows you who they truly are through their own actions, you have the power to decide whether you want them in your life any longer or not. You can always rebuild a positive and healthy relationship based on understanding, acceptance, and honesty through communication- whether it be with the love of your life, with someone not currently in your life or with someone you no longer want in your life.

I WAS ABLE TO FORGIVE MYSELF, MY PARENTS, AND MY FRIENDS. I HAVE THE MOST WONDERFUL RELATIONSHIP WITH MY FAMILY AND I HAVE REBUILT TRUST WITH MY FRIENDS. THESE CONNECTIONS ARE SOLIDIFIED BY MY APPRECIATION FOR THOSE PEOPLE WHO LOVE ME, BECAUSE I NOW ALLOW ME TO LOVE ME, WHICH IN TURN ALLOWS ME TO LOVE THEM BACK.

Exploring Your Soul

chapter three

Standing Apart Brings Us Closer Together

I'VE NEVER QUITE FIT INTO MY SURROUNDINGS. WHEN I WAS YOUNGER, ALL THE KIDS WERE WEARING MATCHING DENIM OUTFITS WITH WHITE SNEAKERS. I, ON THE OTHER HAND, WAS SPORTING YELLOW BELLBOTTOMS AND A PSYCHEDELIC BUTTERFLY-COLLAR BUTTON-DOWN I HAD FOUND AT THE SALVATION ARMY. BELIEVE ME, I FELT LIKE THE COOLEST GIRL IN THAT GET-UP! YES, I ADMIT THAT IT WAS LOUD AND PROBABLY A DESPERATE ATTEMPT FOR ATTENTION BY AN EGO DRIVEN ADOLESCENT. BUT, IT WAS ME. IT WAS WHO I WANTED TO BE, AT LEAST FOR A DAY. THAT OUTFIT AND THE CHOICE I MADE TO STAND OUT SO BOLDLY WAS AN EXPLORATION OF MY TEENAGE-SELF, AND TO SAY THE LEAST, AN EXPLORATION OF MY PREFERRED COLOR PALLET.

I really enjoyed challenging myself to stand apart from the mainstream. I am still that way now, although my style has refined with age and when I go vintage shopping I tend to look for classic signature pieces. From fashion trends, to music, to literature, I like challenging myself with finding a different perspective on life versus following the one that is laid out for me by consumerism. Doing this has helped me understand who I am as an individual and has shown me that I have the courage to stand apart from the crowd, even though I am risking ridicule and judgment to do it. This may sound oddly contradictory coming from a model whose job it is to sell fashion trends that people will follow, but, I believe trends are created in order to enhance style, not dictate it.

I LOVE THE IDEA THAT BY STANDING APART, FORMING MY OWN OPINIONS AND LIVING BY THEM, I AM IN CONSTANT EXPLORATION AND REAFFIRMATION OF MY SOUL. IN DOING SO, I CAN IN TURN CHALLENGE AND ENCOURAGE MY PEERS TO DO THE SAME BY MY EXAMPLE. IN THE END IT ALL COMES DOWN TO LISTENING TO WHAT YOUR HEART AND YOUR GUT IS TELLING YOU. LISTEN CLOSELY, BECAUSE YOUR HEART NEVER LIES.

"Listen closely because your heart never lies."

Studying life - whether art, nature or people have added to this by broadening my perspective even further. Take a moment every day to stop worrying about what errands you have to run or what daily chores you must complete and find something new and interesting to think about. For example, looking at a painting or pondering the change of seasons, even observing another person's actions forces you to broaden your thinking. Step outside of your own thoughts occasionally and wonder what it must be like to be someone else - think what they think, do what they do or have what they have. Ironically, this manner of self-discovery through comparison and 'putting yourself in some one else's shoes' builds empathy and compassion, bringing people closer together. When I put myself in someone else's position, I can relate to that person with greater understanding. Everything I've encountered this way - with compassion, empathy, and an open mind, has shown me how life can be joyous and sad all at once. But that is the beauty in discovering who I am, through understanding how things affect me, and how I choose to react.

Breaking Out Of The Box

In society today, I believe that a large emphasis is put on money, fame, and sexuality. We are taught that within this Holy Trinity lies our power and worth. When in reality, our power lies in who we are as individuals - our actions, our intelligence, our imagination, our creativity, our compassion, and our drive. When I began nurturing these aspects of myself, I realized that I was empowering my own individual beauty and the gift I have to give to the world - the reason I live. Everyone is capable of doing this. We just have to focus our minds on what we feel is important and explore what truly makes us happy, not what we are told should make us happy. This empowers us to discover our own individual beauty.

"our power lies in who we are as individuals"

Our potential as human beings is both wide and extensive, even though I find it natural for people to want to 'box' things (including themselves) into categories

they can easily understand. That's only because people fall into the habit of judging what is unknown based on their personal comfort level with it, rather than having an open mind and using their imagination to see the potential of new ideas. With practice and compassion, we can break the habit of judging before completely understanding something. With that said, I also believe that it is unnatural for people to live a 'boxed-in' life and truly be happy or reach their full potential.

For example, I am not just a dancer, writer, model, or vocalist. I am all of these things. In life, my path changed sev-

ERAL TIMES BEFORE I KNEW TRULY WHAT IT WAS THAT I WANTED TO DO. I ALWAYS FOLLOWED MY HEART, SO WHEN SOMETHING DIDN'T FEEL RIGHT ANYMORE OR I NO LONGER FELT A DRIVING PASSION FOR IT, I MUSTERED ALL MY COURAGE TO MOVE ON TO A NEW CAREER INTEREST. I HAD TO PASS THROUGH FEAR IN ORDER TO GAIN COURAGE SO THAT I COULD MOVE ON AND PURSUE WHAT I TRULY WANTED TO DO NEXT. FEAR IS NATURAL AND EVERYONE EXPERIENCES IT. I WAS AFRAID OF FAILING AT SOMETHING NEW. I WAS AFRAID BECAUSE IT WAS SOMETHING NEW. I WAS AFRAID THAT I WAS FAILING AT WHAT I HAD DECIDED TO MOVE ON FROM. BUT FEAR CAN BE CONQUERED. IT IS NORMAL TO FEEL IT. ONCE I REALIZED THIS I COULD CONTINUE ON TOWARDS MY DREAMS AND ALLOW MYSELF THE SPACE TO GROW INTO MY FULLEST POTENTIAL BY NURTURING ALL THE CREATIVE ASPECTS OF MYSELF.

EVENTUALLY, ALL MY EXPERIENCES AND ALL OF MY CAREER CHOICES ADDED UP TO WHAT I AM TODAY. ALL OF THE PATHS I HAVE TAKEN IN LIFE

"Singing in a rock band has taught

OFFER A BROADER PERSPECTIVE ON THE WORLD AND HAVE AWARDED ME TOOLS THAT HELP ME TO BETTER EXPRESS MYSELF IN MY ART TODAY. BALLET AND DANCE TAUGHT ME MOVEMENT AND GRACE, DISCIPLINE AND CONTROL. WRITING AND POETRY HAS OPENED MY EYES TO THE COLORS OF THE WORLD. MODELING HAS TAUGHT ME POISE AND FASHION, AND HAS ALLOWED ME THE OPPORTUNITY TO GROW INTO MY OWN INDIVIDUAL SENSE OF STYLE. SINGING IN A ROCK BAND HAS TAUGHT ME FREEDOM AND ABANDONMENT.

me freedom and abandonment."

Become Present, We Are Who We Are

When performing, I dissect my soul. I try to be the most honest I can with myself at the very moment I go on stage. I always ask myself, "What am I feeling right now?" Sometimes I'm excited and I feel energetic! Other times I feel angry. Sometimes I just want to disappear. I take these moments with myself to really feel what it is I have going on inside of me because this is who I am. I strive to become present in the moment and not think about the past. I want to allow the future to manifest into something great by giving all I can of myself right now. People, I think, are taught to suppress their emotions in order to maintain a certain social image, or so as to appear in control. But trying to hide our emotions would be futile, because our feelings eventually make themselves known regardless of our efforts to conceal them. Through this, I learn what I most like about myself, and, what dark corners are hidden in my soul. For at least thirty minutes of raw fun on stage I can release my emotions and feel exactly what I want to. I can scream and shout and cry and laugh without any filter.

On stage, or in the artistic medium I have chosen, I don't always have to maintain a sense of 'beauty.' People do not fit into a box of 'niceness.' We are who we are. We are not always happy and we are not always sad. We just are. That's the beautiful thing about humanity - our emotions vary. Performing becomes a process of just being me - happy, sad, angry, excited. It's about simple expression. Everyone can do this without hurting the people around them, or more importantly, the people they love. You just have to find the outlet that works best for you, the one thing in life you cannot live without doing.

> "I want to allow the future to manifest into something great by giving all I can of myself *right now*."

MODEL DIET

chapter four

I LOVE JUNK FOOD! THERE, I'VE SAID IT TO THE WORLD! IF THERE IS ONE BAD HABIT I HAVE IT IS MY PROPENSITY TOWARDS SUGAR AND POTATO CHIPS! I LOVE CUPCAKES AND CANDY, POPCORN, ICE CREAM, CAKE, CHOCOLATE, SODA, AND MOST OF ALL POTATO CHIPS. UNFORTUNATELY, WHEN CONSUMED IN MASSIVE AMOUNTS, THESE FOODS CAN BECOME COUNTER PRODUCTIVE TO THE INTERNAL RELATIONSHIP I HAVE WITH MY BODY. FOOD HAS A DIRECT IMPACT ON THE WAY WE FEEL PHYSICALLY AND EMOTIONALLY. IT IS THE ENERGY WE PUT IN OURSELVES TO HELP OUR BODIES WORK THE MOST EFFECTIVELY. NATURALLY, OUR BODIES WILL REACT TO THE DIFFERENT KINDS OF ENERGY WE FUEL THEM WITH. IT'S REALLY IMPORTANT TO NOURISH YOUR BODY WITH THE RIGHT AMOUNT OF NUTRITIOUS FOODS AND EXERCISE... AND OCCASIONALLY WITH A BIT OF DESERT!

EATING WELL MAKES YOUR BODY FEEL WELL. HEALTHY FOODS PROVIDE VITAMINS AND ENERGY TO HELP YOUR BODY FUNCTION AT ITS BEST. NUTRITIOUS FOODS CLEANSE YOUR BODY, FEED YOUR BODY, AND IN TURN HELP TO CLEANSE YOUR ATTITUDE AND FEED YOUR SOUL. A LOT OF MY FRIENDS AND YOUNG PEOPLE THAT I ENCOUNTER DO NOT LIKE THEIR PHYSICAL APPEARANCE BECAUSE THEY CONSTANTLY COMPARE THEMSELVES TO

Hollywood stars that are extremely lean and glamorous. I'm pretty sure they don't realize that people who work in the entertainment industry have developed strict regiments of exercise, healthy eating, and healthy living in order to maintain their Hollywood physique. This includes personal trainers, hours at the gym or working out, nutritionists, and when on the red carpet, stylists pick out the perfect clothes to compliment their body and skin tone. They also have hair stylists and makeup artists. Now, everyone cannot afford all of this help in becoming "perfect," but we can start by simply taking care of ourselves and eating well.

Once you start eating healthy and working out just a few times per week, I promise that you will feel better about your body and better about yourself. Why do it? Because you deserve it! Plain and simple you deserve to feel better, and to feel good about yourself... just because. Your body will naturally react in a positive way towards a new regime, and you'll be proud of the fact that you've accomplished this positive change. In the end, we can have respect for and an understanding of our own body type. We can build confidence by understanding our own individuality and how we are all made differently.

You don't need a personal trainer or a nutritionist, a stylist or makeup artist to change your life and feel luxurious in your own skin. It's as simple as changing a few things a day concerning how you spend your time awake. My daily routine goes loosely as follows. And I say loosely because it may change slightly day to day, since it is not an overly strict, intimidating diet-and-work-out routine.

Daily Routine: Simple Ways To Feeling Luxurious And Fabulous

Every morning I wake up, drink a full glass of water, and write for an hour. I have had to push myself in waking up earlier to do this because I am naturally a bit lazy and love sleeping in. But I also love writing, so I think the effort is well worth it. Then I work out a little by doing crunches, sit-ups, leg lifts and other simple calisthenics that help me to maintain a lean appearance. I stretch as well, which helps to maintain a limber body and gets oxygen into your muscles. Usually this doesn't take more than 20 minutes. I also love running. Some days I go for a two-mile run to get my blood flowing and to feel strong! Then I hit the shower with a luxurious soap or body wash, because I deserve it.

Dress To Impress... Yourself

Wardrobe is highly important. I usually take my time in getting dressed because I want to pick out the right outfit that properly represents my attitude for the day. It usually boils down to a t-shirt and jeans, but I can dress it up or down, and style it differently depending on the mood I'm in. This usually goes by theme. I could be really rocker with black boots, cut-off shorts and a metal band t-shirt, or really clean and simple with pretty sandals, jeans, a white t-shirt and a nice sweater or blazer. Personal style develops and changes over time. I'm never afraid to try something new, but if it doesn't feel comfortable I take it right back off and go back to plan A. If you feel uncomfortable with a certain outfit in your bedroom, chances are that you'll feel uncomfortable with it throughout the day. I always try to dress myself in something I feel looks really great. To top it off, sunglasses help me to feel fabulous about myself throughout the day, so I normally just throw the usual pair of everyday, Raybans in the bag before leaving the house.

Breakfast

For the first meal of the day, I normally go for a big bowl of Raisin Bran or any other fiber based cereal to get the digestive track going. It is really important to get a good amount of fiber in your diet every day to help cleanse your body of built up toxins and waste. I have always had problematic skin in the form of acne.

Your skin is the largest organ of your body. Next to the liver and kidneys, it helps the most in eliminating waste from your system. When I ate a lot of junk food, my body would purge the toxins through my skin: acne, YUK! Therefore, with a good amount of fiber in my diet, I can help my body eliminate these toxins more efficiently without affecting my skin.

"Personal style develops and changes over time. I'm never afraid to try something new..."

Skin

Our skin is the most important outfit we wear. We must take care of it and treat it well, because this outfit isn't going back in the closet. With modeling, I have had to examine my skin on a day-to-day basis. Some days it is flawless, other days not so flawless. But our skin is organic and will go through different phases. Eating well and drinking water are the most important factors in maintaining healthy skin. Outbreaks are painful. A small note on acne: dairy, a lot of refined sugar, fried foods, and caffeine can trigger an outbreak. Try and avoid these foods for a while until your skin clears. Then gradually add them back into your diet to see which ones affect your skin the most. I highly recommend: "The Prescription For Nutritional Healing," as a reference guide for helping cure skin problems. It is a book that offers natural remedies for any body ailment. My grandmother, who is ninety-five years old, swears by it. She recommended it to me, and after years of trying every over-the-counter acne treatment available, and enduring painful facials, in the end just a simple diet change cured me! Thanks Grandma!

Steaming and sweating is also great for your skin. It opens up your pores and cleanses them of toxins like black heads and dead skin cells. If you happen to be a gym goer, hit the steam room for ten minutes after a good sweaty work-out routine. Otherwise you can simply boil a pot of water and stick your mug right over the steam for a few minutes.

Lunch

For lunch I normally have a lettuce or fruit salad to help round out my diet and get good vitamins inside of me. Water based fruits like watermelon, oranges, and grapes are great as snacks because they fill you up, are full of vitamins, and help to hydrate your body. I'll mix these with some protein like tuna fish or sushi. I try to maintain a mostly vegetarian diet, but proteins are also very important in maintaining your health. They are especially good for your skin as they are filled with Zinc.

Dinner

As for dinner, I try to be flexible but healthy. For example, I will eat beans with quinoa and vegetables. I love kale and I think it is a wonder food! Or I'll have a fresh salad with nuts and friut. I love Mexican cuisine and I'll sometimes cook tacos or veggie flautas. I love watching movies late at night and for a while I was in the habit of eating junk food with the film, just to make it a real

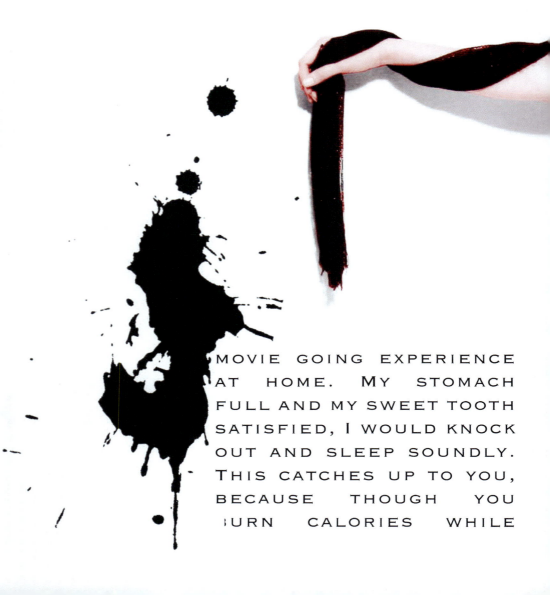

movie going experience at home. My stomach full and my sweet tooth satisfied, I would knock out and sleep soundly. This catches up to you, because though you burn calories while

SLEEPING, IT DOESN'T COMPARE TO THE AMOUNT YOU BURN WHILE AWAKE. NOW I MAKE IT A PERSONAL RULE NOT TO EAT AFTER EIGHT O'CLOCK PM. IF I'M STARVING BY MIDNIGHT AGAIN, I'LL HAVE A GLASS OF WATER, MILK OR JUICE TO SUBSIDE THE HUNGER.

Cooking For Your Stomach And For Your Soul

I think learning to cook is really amazing for the soul. Until I turned twenty-three, I hated cooking. I kept my handbags in the oven and the dishwasher for storage. I would always order in or eat out at restaurants. One day, somehow, I took to cooking and it has caused me to develop a large appreciation for food and the culinary arts. Cooking has helped me strengthen the love and respect I have for my body and my loved ones because now I enjoy preparing delicious foods for myself, and for my family and friends. The first few months were disastrous, but like all things, practice makes perfect. In the end at least it offers an excuse to throw fabulous dinner parties! Make them your own red carpet events!

During the day I am mostly writing music and practicing. I may involve myself in designing and creating a costume for stage performances. Or I may have a photo shoot that I need to model for. After dinner I have rehearsal with my band in our studio, for hours at a time. These activities are strenuous and take a lot of concentration. It's important that I eat well and get some healthy snacks in me throughout the day.

These are all habits I have acquired over the past several years in an effort to rebuild a good relationship with myself, just for me. And they work. As I mentioned before, my daily routine isn't always the same, or so strict. Sometimes I change things up, and not work out at all for maybe two days, or eat breakfast right away and work out later in the day, or treat myself to ice cream and cake a couple of times during the month because I love it so much. We're all human and the idea of always watching your diet and exercise is sometimes overwhelming and frightening. Look at it more as small changes that you can make because you deserve to feel as good as these changes can make you feel! The regiment doesn't have to be strict to be effective.

CUT IT OUT!

I used to smoke a lot! I would wake up, drink coffee and have a cigarette after a night of drinking too much wine. When I began singing professionally, I had to cut all of that out in order to fully utilize my talents, and to really grow as an artist, to become what I have dreamed of becoming. I limit the amount of alcohol I consume when out on the town, and by the way, going out has become a rarity of its own. As much as I have enjoyed cigarettes and coffee in the past, I quit smoking and gave up caffeine regardless. Smoking is simply bad for everyone on so many levels and caffeine dehydrates your body while making you dependent on superficial energy. The best thing I could possibly do to curb this type of debauchery was to drink water, the elixir of life! Water hydrates your body, helps your digestion, cleanses your system, gives you energy, and brings elasticity and a youthful glow to your skin. Dink water!

It can be hard changing. It can sometimes take a year to settle into new habits and a new lifestyle. I still struggle with trying not to over-indulge in my vices such as potato chips, cake, wine and cigarettes! I have had to quit smoking twice! While recording my first full-length album with my first band in early 2009, I made the full commitment to stop smoking completely. And it held for a few months. Then I realized that I would have one cigarette here, one cigarette there. After a while, I realized that I had become an occasional smoker. Which was still bad, if not worst than being a regular smoker. Every time I would occasionally have a cigarette, I could feel it burning my lungs as if I had never smoked before. And the next day, my voice would be raspy and I would be coughing up all kinds of strange things. I had to recommit to my no-smoking way of life. Point being is that with some things, you often have to recommit in your determination toward becoming a better you. It doesn't happen over night, and it's only human to fall out of your routine for a while before recommitting yourself to the good life.

Pamper, Pamper

Beyond healthy eating, exercise, and giving up vices, I highly recommend that everyone take a little time out, at least once a week, to pamper oneself. Some of us can afford to get a massage, but if not, take a hot bath to soak out all of your accumulated stress. Buy a great bubble bath and if you can't afford that, what the heck, throw some shampoo under the running water and you've got bubbles for days! Try to buy a nice soap or body wash that you like. It doesn't have to be expensive. You can find really cheap buys at the local drugstore that are great, as long as you enjoy the smell of it. Once a month, try saving up a little money and go to the salon to get your hair washed, blow-dried and trimmed. I love the process of painting my own nails, but you could also go and get a manicure. Allow yourself to feel luxurious and fabulous. All these things help to build respect and self-worth for your own individual body and spirit, because you're worth it.

chapter five
Rules To Live By

Simple things go a long way. We don't have to be spiritual gurus to be able to live peacefully and harmoniously. The decision we make to better ourselves and our lives starts inside. I've found that these tools can help to turn each and every day in to something amazing!

1. Smile! You'd be surprised at how this little thing can change your whole day.

2. Count your blessings. Think about the things you are appreciative for in life.

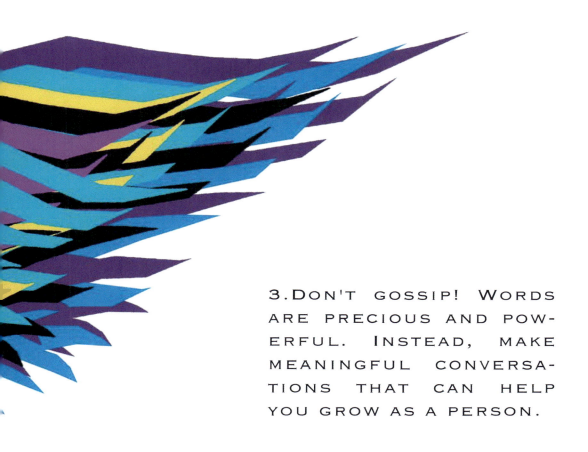

3. Don't gossip! Words are precious and powerful. Instead, make meaningful conversations that can help you grow as a person.

4. Do something everyday that will make you feel more accomplished than the previous day.

5. Think positive and have fun. This sounds easy, but it can be challenging. We often settle into worrying and focusing on the negative aspects of life. With practice you can change this. Every time you feel yourself going into that negative space, just make the decision to turn your thinking around. It takes the world off your shoulders.

6. Find something new and interesting to think about everyday. Never stop learning and broadening your horizons.

7. Become humble. Being confident does not mean being arrogant.

8. Call, email, text or even write a letter to a friend or a family member frequently to tell them you love them. Deepen your relationships with the ones you care about.

9. Do something everyday that will make you feel happy.

10. DRINK WATER! AND BREATHE DEEPLY.

Picture Perfect
chapter six

Believe it or not, I've been modeling since I was thirteen years old. My twin sister Nia Mora, whom at the time was given a camera, fell in love with photography. I, of course, became her subject right away. Nia set up a small photo studio in her room and a darkroom in our basement where she would spend hours laboring over lighting effects and darkroom techniques reminiscent of the great Man Ray (the master of experimental and fashion photography). These were the days when digital photography was still something new. When someone really wanted to know how to become a great photographer, they had to learn lighting and darkroom developing.

There in Nia's modest home studio, we commenced our future careers at the tender age of thirteen without even realizing it. We would shoot together for hours, day after day. Nia would always come up with different creative ideas and themes that challenged me to become different characters within her blossoming fine art photography. We had so much fun learning together and from one another. We both knew that we loved taking photos, she behind the camera and I in front of it. These are some of my most treasured memories. Nia is now an amazing photographer and I have become a well known model. We still shoot together!

Over the past several years since the days of shooting with Nia in our eager adolescence, I have had the opportunity to work with some very talented, professional and amazing artists. Within this time I have had the chance to really hone in on my talent and ambition for becoming a great model. When I first started modeling I can say that I took "nice" pictures. A lot of the time my attempts were tragic, yet earnest. It is only recently that I have become an expert at modeling and understanding the technique and artistry behind it. It took years of photo shoots before I understood how to pose well. Learning this skill took a lot of determination and practice.

Everyday I receive fan mail from young people who live all over the world asking me to take a look at their photos and to give them some advise on posing better. Whether you want to become a professional model or not, it is always helpful to know how to take excellent photos. It is especially important in today's society because our culture has become so image driven. Here are some key tips I've learned in my years of modeling to focus on in order to get great pictures.

Emotion

The camera is not just a devise with a lens, used to take pictures. It is a sensitive instrument expertly handled by the artists behind and in front of it, trained to capture the complete essence of a single moment. All great models understand this and know that to capture the truest form of that moment, you must emote from within. Become present and allow your heart to tell your eyes, face, and body what to do.

Just Relax

Take a deep breath and pretend you are having a conversation with a close friend. A lot of people tend to think posing is this super restricted formula of hands-on-hips and tummy sucked in! Just relax and be yourself. Remember you're beautiful the way you are, and the camera will capture that if you allow it to.

Bathe in the Light

BE VERY MINDFUL OF LIGHTING. REMEMBER THAT PICTURES ARE A TWO DIMENSIONAL REPRESENTATION OF A THREE DIMENSIONAL WORLD. LIGHT ALLOWS THE IMAGE TO EXIST. WITH OUT IT EVERYTHING WOULD BE LEFT IN THE DARK, LITERALLY. WHEN I'M ON SET AT A PHOTO SHOOT, I ALWAYS THINK TO MYSELF "BATHE IN THE LIGHT!" IF YOU BECOME AWARE OF THE PLACEMENT OF YOUR LIGHTING, YOU CAN WORK YOUR ANGLES TO THEIR FULLEST POTENTIAL.

Posing 101

Posing comes down to the individual. Everyone is built differently, so naturally everyone photographs differently. You have to find the poses that work best for your body and know a little bit about what works best for everybody.

Elongate your neck. This creates cleaner lines and helps to frame your face better.

When in doubt, jump. When in the air, your body naturally relaxes.

When sitting, don't sit. Putting all your weight down makes you look sluggish and squashed together. Always lengthen your body and try sitting only half way.

Remember your poise. If you think of how proud you are to be you, your body will naturally take this poised positioning. Shoulders back, chest to the sky!

PRACTICE MAKES PERFECT. USE A MIRROR!

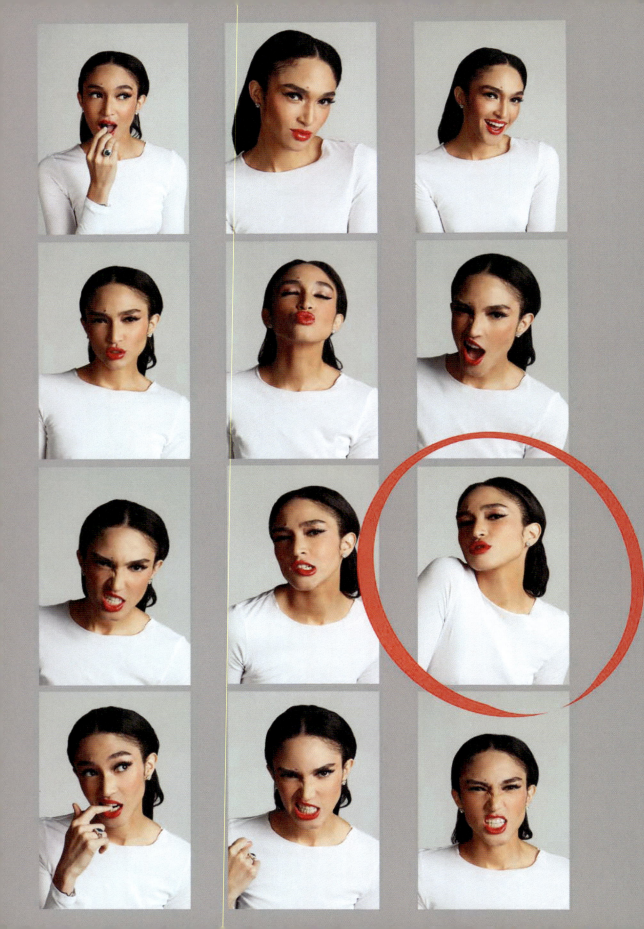

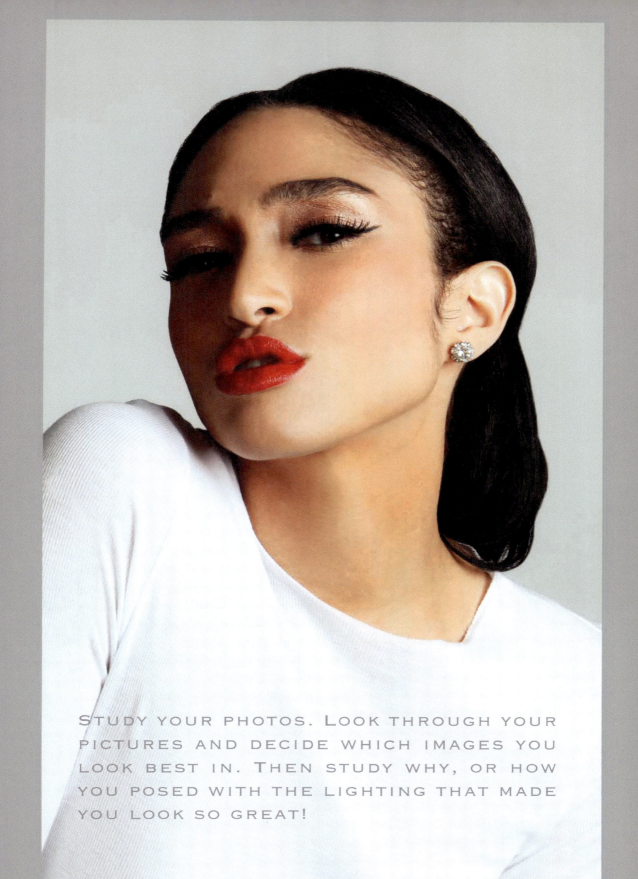

Study your photos. Look through your pictures and decide which images you look best in. Then study why, or how you posed with the lighting that made you look so great!

Be creative. For those who are really striving to become professional models, try doing new things all the time. Don't be afraid to step outside the box and change up the safe poses that you know will work. When I'm on set, I always give photographers a few of these safe poses at first, to makes sure they have at least three strong shots. Then I venture off into a more crazy exploration of movement. Fold in places you normally wouldn't and use your space. Your photographer will let you know which poses work and which ones don't.

Work Your Assets

Plain and simple, work your assets. Pick out the best things you love about yourself and play them up! This varies from person to person. I for example, love showing off my waist, my back and my legs. Become aware of your body and love it! Also, keep in mind that the good side of your face is always the largest side- it photographs better.

chapter seven
For You

While filming America's Next Top Model I had to dig deep and ask myself, "Why do I really want to win this competition?" Of course there were the obvious answers. It would be a dream come true to shoot a spread for Elle Magazine. Even more impressive was the one-year contract to model for Cover Girl and Ford Models. These prizes alone were a very big deal. To win them would be more than I had ever accomplished in my life to date. Wanting anything more may have been asking for too much. But somewhere in my heart I knew there was more to life than momentary success in modeling contracts and magazine spreads. I knew somehow that the real reward would come from inspiring other people to find beauty and confidence within themselves!

With thirty-five girls left in the semifinals, Tyra Banks called me into the judging panel. I vividly remember her asking me, "Why do you want to be a part of this competition Naima?" I answered, "To inspire people like myself." Then she asked me how exactly I planned on inspiring people as a model when most people look at fashion magazines and do not see themselves reflected within the pages? I told her I wasn't sure, but I knew that by living with compassion somehow I could. From that moment on, all the other prizes were only tools and a means to an end.

I have been all over the United States and a lot of the world telling people my story. I'm just a simple girl from a small town who dreams big. I tell everyone I meet to continue working toward their own dreams in order to find true happiness. I see a small resemblance of myself reflected in each person I speak to. The common thread is our humanity, our need for hope and love. So, maybe the answer to Ms. Banks is not whether or not people see themselves reflected in the pages of a magazine, but whether or not people can see themselves reflected in me- and in each other.

My greatest success and most treasured prize has been the opportunity to inspire others in their pursuit of beauty, knowledge, compassion, love, belief and finding creativity within themselves. My hope is that one day you too will be an inspiration to others. Success does not just come from winning a grandiose prize like an internationally syndicated model competition. Success comes in all different ways, shapes and sizes. It comes from having the faith to smile while persevering through your darkest hour, or taking care of a friend in need. Success is also finding harmony within yourself and building harmonious relationships with everyone in your life. Success is having the courage, especially in the face of obstacles, to work really hard in order to make your dreams come true!

CREDITS
COVER SHOOT:
PHOTOGRAPHY BY NIA MORA-MOYNIHAN
FOR MORE WORK BY NIA MORA-MOYNIHAN PLEAS VISIT:
WWW.OPENSEAPHOTOGRAPHY.COM
MAKEUP BY HIYIYATUN MUQARIBU
FOR MORE WORK BY HIYIYATUN MUQARIBU PLEASE VISIT: WWW.HIYIYATUN.COM

TABLE OF CONTENTS:
PHOTOGRAPHY BY DEREK BLANKS
FOR MORE WORK BY DEREK BLANKS
PLEASE VISIT: HTTP://DBLANKS.COM

CHAPTER ONE:
ALL PHOTOGRAPHY BY HOWARD HUANG
FOR MORE WORK BY HOWARD HUANG
PLEASE VISIT WWW.HOWARDHUANG.COM

CHAPTER TWO:
PAGES (21,25,26,30)
PHOTOGRAPHY BY OSWIN BROWNE
FOR MORE WORK BY OSWINE BROWNE PLEASE CONTACT: OZYTRON@HOTMAIL.COM

PAGES (13, 17) PHOTOGRAPHY BY
JEWEL ESTEPHANOS
FOR MORE WORK BY JEWEL ESTEPHANOS
PLEASE VISIT:
WWW.BRIGHTLIGHTMEDIAINC.COM

CHAPTER THREE:
ALL PHOTOGRAPHY BY ERIC MARTIN
FOR MORE WORK BY ERIC MARTIN
PLEASE VISIT: WWW.ERICMARTINPHOTO.COM

CHAPTERS FOUR & FIVE:
ALL PHOTOGRAPHY BY ROMER PEDRON
FOR MORE WORK BY ROMER PEDRON
PLEASE VISIT: WWW.ROMERPEDRON.COM

CHAPTER SIX:
ALL PHOTOGRAPHY BY NIA MORA-MOYNIHAN
FOR MORE WORK BY NIA MORA-MOYNIHAN
PLEASE VISIT:
WWW.OPENSEAPHOTOGRAPHY.COM
MAKEUP BY HIYIYATUN MUQARIBU
FOR MORE WORK BY HIYIYATUN MUQARIBU
PLEASE VISIT: WWW.HIYIYATUN.COM
HAIR BY MARK C. ROWBOTHAM
FOR MORE WORK BY MARK C. ROWBOTHAM
PLEASE VISIT
WWW.MARKCHRISTOPHERSALON.COM

CHAPTER SEVEN:
ALL PHOTOGRAPHY BY
LUKE ALLEN HUMPHREY
FOR MORE WORK BY LUKE ALLEN HUMPHREY
PLEASE VISIT:
WWW.LUKEALLENHUMPHREY.COM

SPECIAL THANKS TO:

TO MY DEAR SISTERS NIA, IFE, AND CRYSTAL FOR ALL YOUR SUPPORT IN MY LIFE. I LOVE YOU DEARLY AND WOULDN'T BE THE SAME WITHOUT YOU. YOU GIVE ME LIFE AND STRENGTH IN SO MANY WAYS.

ELIAS DIAZ V. I CAN NOT TELL YOU HOW MUCH I APPRECIATE ALL THE SUPPORT AND LOVE YOU HAVE GIVEN ME THROUGHOUT MY LIFE.

KATHRYN MATTINGLY THANK YOU SO MUCH FOR ALL THE SUPPORT AND CARE YOU PUT INTO THIS BOOK.

Naima reached international fame and broke into the world of fashion after winning the title of America's Next Top Model as an all time fan favorite. She has landed the covers of and shot spreads for many high profile magazines, walked the runway for some of fashion's top designers, been the face of world known cosmetic lines CoverGirl and Sheer Cover, and made cameos on hit television shows. She has received recognizable awards for exceptional achievement, outstanding leadership, and dedication to improving the quality of life including the Spirit of Detroit Award, the California Legislature Assembly Certificate of Recognition, and the prestigious Key to the City to Cincinnati, Ohio. Naima has also become an international and inspirational public speaker with a presentation at TEDx. She often speaks at highly recognized colleges, schools and universities. With this book she hopes to inspire people towards recognizing their true potential and achieving their hopes and dreams. Naima continues modeling and is currently the lead vocalist of the musical project Galaxy Of Tar. She continues also working as a solo performing musical artist.